WORKBOOK
FOR
ATOMIC HABITS

BUILD GREAT HABITS AND BREAK BAD ONES, MAKE TINY CHANGES WITH REMARKABLE RESULTS.

Jani Venne

Copyright, 2023

Cover By:
Coby Blaze Designs

Forget About Goals, Focus On Systems Instead.

The Quality Of Your Life Depends On The Quality Of Your Habits, With Better Habits Anything Is Possible.

Forward

This workbook accurately accounts for internal stimuli and external emotions that have a direct influence on our development of good habits and elimination of bad habits. Completion of this guide will give you a different perspective of how you view your habits and will generally help you develop a pleasant identity through automated behavioural change.

This Atomic Habit workbook comes with template questions that guide you as you redesign your identity and focuses on modifying the cues available in your environment that trigger certain habits in your current life.

Habit tracking, environment change, partnerships and family hold an important role in motivating our repeated need and want to feel and act different, all these will be tackled in this workbook.

LAW #1
MAKING IT OBVIOUS

When you design your own world, the results of good habits become obvious and visible. You will develop high self-control, awareness of current habits and build an implementation plan to finally replace bad habits with new good ones.

List Current Daily Habits You Want To Get Rid Of:

- ....
- ....
- ....
- ....
- ....
- ....
- ....
- ....
- ....
- ....
- ....
- ....
- ....
- ....
- ....
- ....
- ....
- ....
- ....
- ....
- ....
- ....
- ....
- ....

... all of them!

Now Read Through Your List And Mark Your Habits According to intensity. Example:

1. Good Habit, Write (+) Next To It.
2. Bad Habit, Write (-) Next To It.
3. Neutral Habit, Write (=) Next To It.

All habits serve you in some way, they can only be effective or non effective depending on your goals. Read through this scorecard everyday to make sure you are aware of what needs to be worked on.

Best Way To Start New And Desirable Habits.

List Of Daily Habits You Want To Develop:

- ....
- ....
- ....
- ....
- ....
- ....
- ....
- ....
- ....
- ....
- ....
- ....
- ....
- ....
- ....
- ....
- ....
- ....
- ....
- ....
- ....
- ....
- ....
- ....
- ....
- ....
- ....
- ....

When X happens, I will respond with Y actions. Clarity builds full control and high esteem towards achieving atomic habits.

New Habit:	Day:	Time:	Place:

Example: Daily Workouts (20 min) on [Day] at [Time] in [Place]

Place New Habits At A Time & Place You Consider Most Success.

Always Pick The Right Cue To Kick Things Off When Stacking habits To-gether! Stack Up New Habits You Wish To Manifest.

Finances:

After I....:	I Will...:

Social Skills:

After I....:	I Will...:

Tie Your Desired Habit To Something You're Already Doing Everyday.

Healthy Eating:

After I....:	I Will...:

Exercise:

After I....:	I Will...:

Example: After I [See Stairs], I Will [Take Elevator Instead]

Mood:

| After I....: | I Will...: |

....

....

....

....

....

....

....

....

....

....

....

....

....

Gratitude:

| After I....: | I Will...: |

....

....

....

....

....

....

....

....

....

....

....

....

....

....

Meditation:
After I....:
I Will...:

Marriage:
After I....:
I Will...:

Its easy not to play ball if its tucked away in the closet. Its easier to quit drinking excessive alcohol if you give a purpose to every drinking spree you have. Design your Environment for success.

What Changes You'd Make Around You To Influence New Habits?

....
....
....
....
....
....
....
....
....
....
....
....
....
....
....
....

How Will The Changes Benefit You?:

....
....
....
....
....
....
....
....
....

Habits are easier to change in new environments. Escape subtle triggers and cues that nudge you to current habits. The context usually becomes the cue with practice. Trying to be more creative? Switch to a bigger room or outdoor space. Trying to eat healthier? Try shopping from a different store to avoid instant triggers in the current habits.

Each Context Should Be Associated With A Particular Habit.

What Benefits Will New Environments Have On:

Your Relationships?

Your Personality?

Work / Business / Finances?

Instead of using Willpower every time you are faced with a new temptation, better use your energy to optimizing your new environment. Self-control is not a long term strategy, Its easier to avoid temptations once or twice.

Rather than making it obvious, make bad habits invisible.

Cut Off Bad Habits At The Source By Reducing Exposure To Cues That Cause It.

How Will You Avoid Tempting Situations:

In Your Finances?

In Your Personality / Relationships?

In Your Healthy Eating?

How Will You Avoid Tempting Situations:

In Your Work Environment?

In Your Daily Workouts / Fitness?

In Your Other Situations?

LAW #2
MAKING IT ATTRACTIVE

Making a habit attractive increases the odds of its occurrence., develop a Dopamine effect on your habit before you experience it and not after. Your motivation to act spikes as your dopamine increases in anticipation on your new habit. Pairing an action you want with an action you need can make your new habits more attractive, fun and exciting as anticipation of rewards gets you to take action. The more attractive an opportunity is, the more likely it is to become habit-forming.

In Your Work Environment?

In Your Daily Workouts / Fitness?

In Your Relationships / Family?

In Your Marriage?:

In Your Personality?

In Your Other Situations?

To Make Rewards More Attractive What Activities Will You Associate With New Habits?

In Your Work Environment?

....
....
....
....
....
....
....
....
....

In Your Daily Workouts / Fitness?

....
....
....
....
....
....

In Your Relationships / Family?

....
....
....
....
....
....
....
....
....
....
....

In Your Marriage?:

In Your Personality?

In Your Other Situations?

Now Lets Bundle Your Temptations With Stacks Of Habits.

After I [Current Habit]	I Will [Habit I Need]

In Your Work Environment?

In Your Daily Workouts / Fitness?

In Your Relationships / Family?

In Your Marriage?:
After I [Current Habit]
I Will [Habit I Need]

In Your Personality?

In Your Other Situations?

After I [Habit I Need]	I Will [Habit I Want]

In Your Work Environment?

In Your Daily Workouts / Fitness?

In Your Relationships / Family?

After I [Habit I Need]	I Will [Habit I Want]

A Genius Is Not Born But Educated And Trained.

With Deliberate Practice And Development Of Good Habits a Child Can Become A Genius In Any Field.

Instead of using Willpower everytime you are faced with a new temptation, better use your energy to optimizing your new environment. Self-control is not a long term strategy, Its easier to avoid temptations once or twice.

Rather than making it obvious, make bad habits invisible. Join a crowd of which your desired behavior is normal to them.

- Proximity -

What Good Habits Are You Imitating From Those Close To You?

- Conformity -

What Good Habits Are You Imitating From The Many (Community) ?

- Admiration -

What Good Habits Are You Imitating From The Powerful?

LAW #3
MAKING IT EASY

Trying to find the optimal plan for change can be bogging, focused on figuring out the best approach that we never get to take action. When you are in motion you are busy strategizing and planning, no results yet. Action on the other hand has an outcome, that's the difference between being in Motion and taking Action. Repeating a habit leads to clear physical modifications in the human brain. "Neurons that fire together wire together" - Hebb's Law.

Walk Slowly But Never Backwards.

To Fully Automate A New Habit You Need To Take Action Everyday, How Long It Will Take Is Of Less Important. Focus On Action And Not Being In Motion.

The amount of time spent on forming a habit is less import compared to the number of times you need to perform the habit.

What New Habits Do You Need To Take Action Starting Today With least Planning And No Duration?

In Your Marriage?	Frequency?

In Your Personality?

In Your Other Situations?

In Your Work Environment?

New Habit	Frequency?

In Your Daily Workouts / Health / Fitness?

In Your Relationships / Family?

Reduce friction associated with new, good habits, this will make it easy for you to perform them. On the hand increase friction required to perform current bad habits, the higher the friction the more difficult it becomes to take action. To prime for a healthy diet week, chop tons of fruits and vegetables on weekend and place in containers to make then ready to eat through the week.

How Do You Intend To Prime Your Environment With Reduced Friction On Good Habits And Increased Friction On Bad Ones:

In Your Marriage?
Frequency?

In Your Personality?

In Your Other Situations?

In Your Work Environment?

Frequency?

In Your Daily Workouts / Health / Fitness?

In Your Relationships / Family?

New Habit	Two-Minute Decision
Example: Do Thirty Minutes Of Yoga	**Take Out My Yoga Mat**

Most habits happen at decisive moments, a fork in the road that can either lead to a productive day or unproductive one. Develop rituals at the start of every habit to help you get in a state of deep focus.

For increased focus or productivity you can choose to turn off group chat and notification, delete social apps and games from you phone except your game console. You could move to a friendlier neighbourhood for increased happiness, etc.

In Your Healthy Eating

....

....

....

....

....

....

....

....

In Your Work / Productivity

....

....

....

....

....

....

....

....

In Your Finances

....

....

....

....

....

....

....

....

In Your Personality

In Your Marriage / Relationships

In Your Environment

LAW #4
MAKING IT SATISFYING

The Cardinal Rule Of Behavioural Change Is Not Knowledge But Consistency. Knowing What To Do, How, When And Not Doing It Has Little Or No Influence On Your Adoption Of New Habits, Make Habit Adoption Pleasurable. Less Satisfying Experiences Give Us Little Reasons To Repeat Them, Brushing Your Teeth With Unflavoured Toothpaste. This Chapter Completes The Habit Loop By Seeing To It That You Repeat You New Habits With A Level Of Satisfaction.

In Your Work Environment?

In Your Daily Workouts / Fitness?

In Your Relationships / Family?

In Your Personality?

In Your Finances?

In Your Work Environment?

In Your Daily Workouts / Fitness?

In Your Relationships / Family?

In Your Personality?

In Your Finances?

New Behaviours Stick If They Are Pleasurable, How Do You Intend To Make These New Behaviours Satisfying:
Instant Gratification

In Your Work Environment?

....

....

....

....

....

In Your Daily Workouts / Fitness?

....

....

....

....

In Your Relationships / Family?

....

....

....

....

....

In Your Personality?

....

....

....

....

In Your Finances?

....

....

....

....

In Your Work Environment?

In Your Daily Workouts / Fitness?

In Your Relationships / Family?

In Your Personality?

In Your Finances?

Make Progress Satisfying With Visual Measures.

This Will Reinforce Your Behaviour And Will Add Immediate Satisfaction To Any Of Your Activities.

For Instance you place two jars, one with 100 marbles another empty. Each time you complete a task you then move one marble to the empty jar till the empty jar becomes full, this can be practiced everyday to help keep your habits on track.

Tracking Your Habit is powerful because it leverages all laws of behavioural change.

In Your Work Environment?

....

....

....

....

....

In Your Daily Workouts / Fitness?

....

....

....

....

In Your Relationships / Family?

....

....

....

....

....

In Your Personality?

....

....

....

....

In Your Finances?

....

....

....

....

BENEFITS

#1 Tracking Makes It Obvious.
Recording your actions initiate a trigger to perform the next one and keeps you honest.

#2 Tracking Makes It Attractive.
A subtle reminder that you are making progress, that the best form of motivation.

#3 Tracking Makes It Satisfying.
It feels amazing to watch your results grow, the size of your investment portfolio, signs of abs, length of your manuscript,etc. Feeling good about your habits helps you endure the process.

Tracking isn't for everyone, and there is no need to measure your entire life. But nearly anyone can benefit from it in some form— even if it's only temporary.

In Your Work Environment?

In Your Daily Workouts / Fitness?

After I finish each set at the gym,   I will record it in my workout journal.

In Your Relationships / Family?

In Your Personality?

In Your Finances?

So Far Which New Habits Have You Failed To Follow Up? Due To Life Interruptions, emergencies, etc.

- ....
- ....
- ....
- ....
- ....
- ....
- ....
- ....
- ....
- ....
- ....
- ....

Never Miss Twice! How Do You Intend To Recover From The Break Down In Behaviour.

- ....
- ....
- ....
- ....
- ....
- ....
- ....
- ....
- ....
- ....
- ....
- ....

Reclaiming you broken habit makes failing re-
dundant, successful people rebound quickly soon
as they fail despite having a bad day, perfor-
mance or workout. Everyone gets kicked down
by life but those who kick back always win.

Give Yourself An Immediate Reward When A Habit Is Completed.

||||||||||||||||||||||||||||||||||||||||||||||||||||||||||||||||||||||||

Small habits don't add up. They compound.
That's the power of atomic habits. Tiny changes.
Remarkable results.

Thank you for taking your time to making
"YOU" that better person, we hope you enjoyed
our guide to James Clear's Atomic Habits, get a
copy if you haven't already and looking forward
to your new behavioural success.

Make Yourself Whom You Wish To Be!

||||||||||||||||||||||||||||||||||||||||||||||||||||||||||||||||||||||||||||||||

THE END